BREATHING BLESSED AIR LLC

For inquiries on self-publishing your own
book contact Breathing Blessed Air LLC at
breathingblessedair@yahoo.com

T. Usama Shabazz

Tug of War
My Road to the Most High

- Table of Contents –

Introduction

Due to all the ups and downs I went through in life;
I've always felt God had a plan for me that I never
really understood. Why me? Just like in the Bible, or
any God inspired book that someone has written to
honor God, but also show the world that there will be
many ups and downs on your road to God. Everyday
people like you and I struggle with sin, some more
than others. The key is knowing without God it is
impossible to live a truly satisfying life, so we have to
continue to put God in our lives, no matter the
circumstances.

When you read people's books or the Bible, you see
that it's a reason that God encourages us to read these
types of stories. God shows us that we're not the only
ones going through these situations, and people from
the Bible, up to modern day times have gone through

similar situations and overcame them by the grace and mercy of God alone.

Me seeing evil at an early age opened my mind to the reality of God and Satan, however, it still didn't prevent me from the sins I chose to do willingly. Moreover, it did show me that God forgives, and He is readily open to forgive and assist us. I wrote this book to encourage others, and myself about how Satan will continue to pull us down in life. Please, don't ever assume that God has turned His back on you, and certain situations.

God has allowed us to be in certain situations whether we like it or not, those trials were needed for us at that appointed time, and even if we didn't see it then, God is All-Knowing. Like some of the people in the Bible, it took forty plus years to see God's plan for their life. It took for my life to be on the line to really see what God was trying to show me during my own personal journey to Him. As I strive to give myself to him fully, I also will share my story in hopes of reaching those choosing to get closer to God, and also choosing to share their stories as well, with hopes of healing, restoration and all of us coming closer to him and changing for the better. God-Willing

Understanding Evil At An Early Age

Many people think of horror movies, or books when the subject of monsters and demons comes up, but not me. When I was four years old staying at an apartment complex (as we like to call it, the projects), me and my brother Howard shared a room and bed together. Just like any normal big brother, my older brother Howard would say things to scare me when our mother would turn off the light and close the bedroom door. Soon he would start telling me scary things I would be left awoke to look around in the dark with the feeling that something demonic was looming in the darkness watching my every move. At first, I would see ultra lighted orbs in the corner of our bedroom, and the bedroom door. The more nights passed by, the bigger the mysterious orbs would grow. From a baseball shaped orb, to what looked to me like a trench coat and hat with no legs on the ground, or face in between the hat and coat. It never moved from the corner but would interact and mimic my hand gestures, frightening right? At this time in my life, the famous game to play was to act like I'm shooting a gun at this thing, and it would do the same thing back, but never would move. It's like even while asleep, something would make me open my eyes around three o'clock in the morning with this entity already there watching me, but never moving from the corner of my bedroom.

The more time passed, it befriended me, and the more comfortable I got seeing it at night. The more nights of seeing it, I began having the same nightmare almost every night of a witch chasing me through the apartment we lived in somehow, I always ran and hid under the same car in front of our apartment complex. While watching the legs of the witch walk around to the car I was hiding under and stop in front of me, bend over and look at me, and as soon as I saw the tip of the witch hat bow down. I would jump up out of my sleep right before seeing the witch face. While just thinking it was a nightmare, my mother would talk and comfort me and send me back to bed, but the nightmare was the only dream I seem to have nowadays.

As soon as the weather got warm outside, my mother would let us open the window to let a little air in our room, due to it being so hot outside. It seemed like I would be in a deep sleep and would awaken suddenly with my eyes looking automatically towards the window, to see the witch levitating on something looking me dead in my eyes. As young as I was, I would pull the covers over my head and wake my older brother up. Howard would always look when it was too late. One night about three in the morning, I woke up to see the witch there in the window again. This time when I nudged my brother, it seemed like he had already knew because when I nudged him he lightly whispered back "I see it too". We always screamed for our mother who would come running but it would already be gone.

The third demons we saw were about ankle high and always came out when we were already asleep. We would be awakened by hearing them moving around knocking stuff over, talking to one another in a language we didn't understand. They did not like to be seen, and if we moved around, they would stop moving and then when we stop moving, they would start to move around again. Sharing a single bed, my arms would sometimes hang off the bed right above the floor. I would wake up in the morning to see what seemed to be teeth marks on my wrist and hands, the size that was smaller than a baby's tooth. Night after night we would see one of the three demons consistently.

One night while asleep, the entity in the corner revealed its true identity to me while trying to get me to go with it. After seeing it, I began to scream and my mother and her boyfriend happen to be close enough this night to come in our room to witness this entity, soon as they opened the door, the entity took off in between them and disappeared down the hallway and never visited us again showing itself physically. Years later, I've gotten older, my mother refreshed my memory to some of the things I didn't remember that night. She told me the entity and the light kept telling me that it wanted me to go with it, and by it revealing its true identity, that's made me scream.

The nightmare I was always having, might have derived from me disappearing one night, and while my entire family and strangers searched for me frantically, I was found underneath a car, appearing to be hiding and asleep. This would just be the beginning of the beginning of many visions and entities showing themselves to me, letting me know it is more to life than what meets the eyes. I thought to myself, if demons exist on Earth, then so does a God in Heaven!

Living in Hell on Earth As a Child

I grew up in a community called Beecher, on the borderline of Flint, Michigan. This neighborhood used to pride itself on community love and togetherness, but during the early 80s, drugs and gang violence ruled king in Beecher. Our loving community as well as Flint, took ten steps backward. Crack cocaine along with heroin, and liquor stores were on every other corner. The pawn shops just about made our communities become a Death Valley. People began getting addicted to local drugs and alcohol, but also losing their jobs and selling all of their belongings. Hanging around the Corner stores and neighborhood corners was where drug dealers marked their territory. Eventually, crime took control of the surrounding cities also. Poverty chased franchise businesses away, the companies kept jobs in the inner city, not anymore!

Eventually gang violence deteriorated what was left of what held our communities together. I grew in this madness, where it seems like every year, it was getting worse and worse. Many of the youth, me being included, begin to hang in these treacherous streets. The streets had nothing to offer us but drugs, alcohol, and violence. Growing up fatherless, all I had was a caring mother who did all she could to provide for me and my brothers Paul, Leon, and Howard. I was the youngest at this time before my brother Shawn was born, I seem to be more serious about life at this time. My mother got us what we needed, and not what we wanted most of the time, meaning not much money circulated through our household, but she spoiled us whenever possible. Seeing children with the latest clothes and shoes, made me want these things I did not have the money to afford. This is one reason I began stealing at an early age and couldn't be trusted around stuff. I wanted so badly to hang with a crew of friends from my neighborhood, committing acts of violence on people from opposing neighborhoods. It had gotten so bad that we resorted to breaking into homes in our own community.

The more poverty stricken the community got, the more dyer everything became. People throwing trash everywhere, strong urine smells everywhere, abandoned buildings everywhere, people addicted to drugs and alcohol walking around looking half dead, like walking zombies, to it eventually looking like hell on earth, and the atmosphere of Beecher became hell on earth.

Drugs and Alcohol

CHAPTER 3

When you look around the world, you'd be surprised to see that most of the world spends a lot of time in a form of intoxication. Everyone from people who work hard, to people doing nothing, spending some or most of their day doing some form of drugs, (street or prescription drugs), and alcohol. You would have to ask yourselves, "Why does a so-called God fearing world, out do themselves to keep people from all walks of life from using drugs and alcohol? A world where they will lock people up in jail for selling drugs, and then, turn around and allow big pharmaceutical companies to constantly prescribed highly addictive drugs. Moreover, they advertise drugs, day and night for our children to see; By television, magazines, billboards, radio and hotlines, etc...

These drugs that these companies give people have many different side effects, even death. You never hear about any of these company owners going to jail, only fined, but what is a fine, after they have generated billions of dollars off the people for years. All they do is payback some of the money they made off the people in lawsuits, all while still selling their products.

Take "the marijuana situation," for instance. People have been imprisoned for years for selling it illegally, only for the same government to allow businesses to operate legally and be taxed on it. The transition from locking up citizens to selling it themselves is crazy, right?

Poverty in the Mind

CHAPTER 4

Similar to what happened with alcohol in prohibition, and as soon as the rich won over politicians, now it's sold legally everywhere, even though it kills you slowly. The age limit of people using drugs and alcohol is getting younger and younger. The government will lock you the minute they catch you trying to make a living selling it though. Who's really the hypocrites for selling drugs and alcohol? I'll let you be the judge.

I used to wonder why you see other places that seem to be mini paradises, that never seem to have the effects of the inner city, but as you get wiser to the game, you realize that it's some form of evil design to make it such. I know many will say, "Oh here we go with this conspiracy theory stuff," but is it really a theory? During the early 60's up to the present (2024), began a serious rise in drugs in urban cities, meaning places of poverty, and different races of poor people. All over the United States, the same situation is going on due to the same strategic designs that effected every urban city, or poverty stricken place around the world. Any time you have poverty stricken people with drug and alcohol addiction, they are readily available and sold on every street corner. You can just about figure out the inevitable outcomes are.

Not just street drugs are the problem, you have legitimatized drug dealers, such as the pharmaceuticals companies, who are turning people into drug addicts also. The street drugs heroin, cocaine, oxytocin, LSD, are the same drugs put into pills forms, liquid uppers and downers. What they don't tell you is that these so-called drugs they're giving us not only messes with the brain, but also your physical and mental capacity, hormones balance, and many times, outright destroy the body. Withstanding things like this poisoning your mind in poverty stricken places, the outcome is chaotic. Now it's reached the suburbs, it's labeled a terrible epidemic, when it's been happening in the inner urban cities for years. Poverty destroys the mind, body and soul, that's why so many do anything to escape this lifestyle. If you keep a people in a dead state of mind, it becomes the physical sooner or later.

Whispers in My Mind

---∞---

CHAPTER 5

As a teenager, I started noticing voices in my mind when it was time to do something I know I ain't have no business doing. Some people call it a gut feeling (meaning your spiritual intuition), or the famous one from the cartoons, with the angel on one side, and the devil on the other. Not knowing it was a deeper meaning to this subject at matter. The worse my temper and pettiness grew, I went from having a angel on one side, and the devil on the other, to just flat out negative, destructive, and chaotic things. I enjoyed the wrong doing, stealing, robbing, gang violence, selling drugs etc... This could be seen inside and out, physically and mentally. I became so low that nothing bothered my conscious at all.

After being shot at age 15, then stabbed the following year at Flint's bus terminal. I became out of control, the state attempted to take me from my mother, but she signed me up for Job Corps, the Judge allowed me to try that. A few months of that, I took off and left job corps to continue my crime spree, up until being arrested again. Before the same Judge I stood, seeing if I was going to juvenile, or released because I was turning seventeen that year. I gave her the same bull crap story every criminal says, that if I'm released, I promise to do the right thing. She looked me in the eyes and told me that it didn't matter if I was telling the truth or not, but the next time I got in trouble, it would be prison I was facing due to me turning seventeen. I left the court room smiling as if I had won the lottery!

A heavy weight crook, what really hurt me was to see

my mother face looking at me like I was the devil himself, cause she knew the falsehood I was speaking about was a lie. She told me when we got in the car to tell her where I'm going, cause I wasn't able to stay at her home anymore. I was a handful, I stayed getting into confrontations with people. She knew I had a death wish on me, and refused to witness me destroy myself, it hurt but deep inside I knew she was dead on point! That is exactly what I had become, so I told her to drop me off at the store so I could run loose through the concrete jungle that possessed me mentally.

Not having my mother's influence in my ear to speak positive things to me, I was left roaming the streets with no guidance. Nowhere to stay, nothing to eat, like a savage I stole food to eat, robbed for money, and slept in abandoned apartments where I grew up in, drinking cheap wine and forty ounces malt liquor. Me and my crew got into it with the new task force armed security that was put out in the villa, due to crime in the apartments. One security guard had a 12 gauge pistol grip pump hanging down in his hand, and for no reason at all, a loud clear voice said take it, and like a robot I told my friend I'm getting ready to snatch this shotgun. After snatching the shotgun, I turned my back and ran towards the back of the apartments. After getting away, I calmed down and got to questioning myself to why I did it in the first place. I woke up the next day not even remembering taken it until a friend let me know and told me to get off the streets cause all the police and task force were looking for me. As low as I was, I refused to sit still, I ran the streets savagely on the run from police, and woke up on homecoming Friday telling my homeboy S-Runn that I needed to get up on some money for homecoming game night. While they were in school, I broke in a house and got caught by police who were happy to see me cause they were already looking for me for taking the gun. While sitting in the County Jail awaiting trial, my mother came and visited me and told me she prayed that I might have my life spared by the Most High by locking me up instead of me dying on the streets. I became a real thug, which was like a demonic creature with no remorse. Even though the Judge didn't want to lock me up cause I was seventeen, he felt just like my mother did, that being locked up would save my life, so at seventeen, he sentenced me to 4-15 years in the State Penitentiary.

Prison Save My Life

CHAPTER 6

Whenever you tell a person that prison saved my life, the look on they face tells it all. The average person can't understand what a person really means when they say these words, "prison saved me". There are many categories listed to why a person would say prison saved them, when really you've heard the stories plenty of times, but did you pay attention, or even care enough to even think why the person is saying it. You got people who were saved by being taken away drugs, alcohol, crimes, killing, people trying to kill them, or all of the above. Some people came to this understanding cause they spiritually knew that the Most High was saving them from something, and deep within prison they found out what. Even in the Holy Scriptures, it tells you some of the Prophets were incarcerated for a safe healing, in order for the Most High to give them some form of spirituality. Whether to save them, or open their eyes to a higher form of spirituality.

Although some people get saved without getting their spiritual eyes opened while incarcerated. Me going to prison forced me to look at all the things I was doing wrong, and actually how close to an animals behavior I had gotten. I didn't know at the time that if The Most High didn't restrain me from myself, that I had chose to run down one road only, and this was a road of destruction, and if The Most High didn't intervene in my life, that I was going to be killed, or I was gonna end up killing somebody else. I was at the lowest of the low, and The Most High save me by taking me out the madness, madness some aren't blessed to make it out of. All praise is due to The Most High, he chose to save me.

TUG OF WAR

Struggling With Self in Prison

CHAPTER 7

Going to prison at the age of seventeen was like getting sentenced to hell. Being taken away from everything, family, friends, the precious daughter Andreada, who was just born. Even though I was still a child mentally, I knew I was going to a man's world, were everything was gonna be a lot more serious, and dangerous. I went in angry like it was everybody problem in the world but mine. Being put in a one man cell in quarantine was like throwing fuel on a fire. After coming to my senses of blaming everybody for me going to prison, and alone in this dark room, then I began to shun myself for doing all the senseless stuff I've done to even be in here, even thinking about the daughter I had left fatherless do to the things I'd done. Would she get to know me? Would she even want too, by the time I get back out? All these things enter your mind. It's like your own conscious torments you, but at the same time, it's when you begin actually start talking to The Most High due to you being in a hellish state with nobody to help you mentally and spiritually.

Like the Most High always wanted, it makes you come to him in submission and humility, humbling yourself. It was like something was beginning to show me that this was the plan the whole time, and I needed to be taken away from what was going to be my very destruction, and save the very soul I was on the verge of losing. Being put in prison population was a test of improving myself also, to being around a multitude of people going through the same thing as me, and some even worse. Everyday was like battling your surroundings, and your own state of mind. Dealing with people in the world who have problems you can't help or solve, but it still becomes a distraction on you trying to get yourself together, so this creates a form of chaos along with all the problems you've accumulated. It becomes another way for Satan to ease in unless you learn to ask The Most High to intervene. Hesitantly I did, and The Most High answered.

Messengers of God In Prison

CHAPTER 8

All throughout the holy scriptures, you hear about messengers of God, that are sent to a people, or just a person. Sometimes it's a warning or some times its to bring you closer to God, coming through a person to show you the way. A lot of people assume you're talking about angels when you mention the word messenger of God, but any type of scripture will tell you a messenger can be an angel or a person guided by the Most High. A messenger means someone coming with a message about something, and when they come, you never know from where, or why they came to you. Like The Most High said, nobody will know the hour or the times, but when you're ready and willing, you will find that The Most High is already steps ahead of you. Making preparations to meet you half, or most of the way.

When I got to prison, spirituality was the only thing I was seeking, cause everything else seemed to be the same old stuff you've seen in the streets, people hustling, fighting, stealing, killing, and homosexuality. Regardless of the madness in prison, God always seems to find the ones who are on a spiritual journey, which I was. Enlightened people from all walks of life seem to have positive inspiration for me, like they knew what I was seeking without me displaying it. The books people would recommend would find its way to me without me seeking it. So I would constantly read and study religion, history, and ancient history. I could go to another prison and someone with these same traits would still find me, constantly feeding my hunger for spirituality, to the point were most of the company I surrounded myself with were God inspired people leading me to a higher consciousness.

God Opened My Eyes in Prison

CHAPTER 9

Everybody has their own view on when they say God opened their eyes and revealed something to them, and how. The reason being is that everyone has their own road and connection to The Most High, which makes y'all connection unique in its own way. Mine, however, was more instinctive and spiritual. When I say opened my eyes, I mean I started seeing things differently in things, people, words, and behavior. A new road in life, never known to me before, which was a positive road, by avoiding the frame of mind I had before, that seemed to box me in from worldly thinking, and spiritual thinking, meaning barely thinking at all. From thinking and behaving like an animal, to finally thinking like a human being, to living as such, mentally, physically, and spiritually.

Many Religions &
One Soul

CHAPTER 10

When you're in prison finding a religion to your liking is like picking what classes you want for college. You have different branches of Christianity, Islam, gangs, White Supremacy Groups, Native American Ritual groups, Civil Rights Groups, Black Supremacy Groups, and plain ole career criminals, who plan on doing the same ole Thing when they get released, without shame. Like college, you see scouts running around finding new inmates to add to their congregation, opening people's minds to things they've never been introduced to before.

Even though a lot of these groups disagree with each other, they try not to step on each others toes when it comes to teaching people, who end up getting in one these groups way of thinking and beliefs. Most of the time they talk behind other groups back to prove who's right or wrong. You would never think trying to save your soul would be so difficult, you will be spread out into so many categories by people who are supposed to be on the same road to elevation as you, and Satan knows this. Satan uses it to his advantage by separating religion.

Religion & Hate

With so many religions in this world, you would think that the world would be a positive paradise, but in our world, it's the total opposite. Everybody thinks their religion is the only true way to get to heaven, nobody has taken the time to think, or understand what's truly missing in this picture. When you look around the world, every religion forms a congregation mainly saying they come in peace, but the opposite of peace is what we wake up to daily. Every individual religion has another religion to look down on, as if they're putting themselves on some higher degree than the rest. In prison, the same egotistic behavior erupts. When I started my road to find religion, I looked for something more in tune with the mental state of mind I wanted, and not needed. I already knew about Christianity, from times of going to church with my mother, but it just didn't get to me at mentally or spiritually at the time.

I began talking to Muslim brothers I jailed with and was invited to a black Muslim meeting given by The Nation of Islam, which was started by the Honorable Elijah Muhammad, with famous members such as Muhammad Ali and Malcolm X. The energy I got was of feelings more personal than spiritual. They were talking about how the white man is the devil, (a grafted being Ade from us), and how we are the original man of the earth, and that's why white people constantly kill and enslave all people of color with melanin. At this time these things interested me, especially how I felt inside about why white people acted so evil toward black people. They also taught black people how to overcome inferiority, a state of mind black people seem to be stuck in. These were things you did not ever hear in the hood, like staying clean (drug-free), cleaning yourself up, eat right, study self, improve self, have love for your brother man and sister, owning your own businesses, take control of your own community.

All these things took my mind to a higher state, but the anger it gave me, tore me down to a lower state of being, instead of spiritual growth. I became angry and prideful against who I felt and knew to be an open enemy. After joining I wrote my family about the new knowledge that I attained and received letters back from my mother, and aunt Pearl, who loved the fact that I was aiming at working towards a higher spirituality, but not by earning it off negativity and hate. Like Malcolm X, I eventually left the Nation of Islam, even though I agreed with a lot the Nation of Islam had to offer, it's like my soul yearned for something more, so my journey continued, so I could find something more soulful, not hateful, on my own road to The Most High.

Hate From Within Self

Without religion, I found myself angry about a lot of things in prison, mostly things from the world I was taken away from. Hearing problems on the phone, or letters from family, friends, and girlfriends, who tell you problems that touch your mind and soul in ways that seem to try and break you. Anger can do a lot of things to you on your road to a higher spirituality. I fought so hard to keep my sanity daily, with up and down relationships, problems you can't help with, watching my daughter grow up in pictures, and not real life. It's like Satan would wait for you to feel good, and then he'd tear it apart before my very eyes. I hated the world inside and a lot of times, you could see my mental thoughts start to appear in my physical being.

If I wasn't careful, I would allow myself to do something stupid, and dig myself down a deeper hole than I am already in. I started praying to God for answers and healing, from the mental pain I was enduring, and once again, The Most High answered my prayers.

Humility

CHAPTER 13

Going all I went through in prison, and at the age I was, I learned a lot, developed a lot of anger, but The Most High sent people to me constantly, to help me stay on my spiritual journey. I met a brother named Faraaaz, who was quiet and laid back, he used to watch me debate with others about religion, history, and many other things. He used to tell me I was fiery meaning (wild and angered easily), but he liked the fact that I liked to read books and learn. One day while talking, he opened up his locker to reveal a gang of books, a treasure full. As soon as I started asking about them, he shut his locker after grabbing one he felt I was ready for, so I took it back to my cell and read thee whole book in one night, and when I brought it back! He was like man, you didn't read that book that fast, I said yes, I did. So, he quizzed me on it.

After telling him about the whole book, he was like man your comprehension and learning on point. We begin walking the yard and studying together on everything from religion, history, and ancient history, to books about things that would blow your mind. Things that even religion couldn't inform you on, like histories I've never heard about before. Knowledge that some of The Holy Books got information from, all over the world that taught self discipline along with forms of religions combined to make you humble yourself in humility. It was a way to become the spiritual person, and not just reading about these types of people. Faraaaz became my teacher with the guidance of The Most High, teaching me to perfect myself spiritually on becoming what we were studying. Instead of the short tempered angry person I was, I started becoming more humble and peaceful, saying words only when time, and only if it's worth saying. Through God, I found a way of life totally different then the craziness of the streets, I found humility amongst The Most High, and before I knew it, I was on my way home on parole, after 5 and half years.

Released to a Chaotic World

CHAPTER 14

The best feeling in the world is being released from prison. You feel so rejuvenating and fresh and clean within, it's like you're starting over in life with a whole new beginning, and a new chapter in your life. Away with the old, and in with the new. Your brain is filled with all the positive aspects you've thought about your whole bit. As you leave prison, you have the full armor of God over you, and then you enter the very hell, you were taken from. In the so-called ghetto, people get a lot of attention drawn to them when they get out, like a form of being a celebrity. Everybody running up to you, hugging you, wanting

50

TUG OF WAR

you to ride with them, telling people on the phone your out, people telling you to come by. Then the sad versions of stories begin to be told to you, like who died, who was on drugs, who locked up, who done had children, and by whom. Taking all this in makes your emotions stir up and down, but you try not to let these things interfere with the joy of you being free. The more you see, the more you realize that the streets you've been taken away from haven't just changed, but they've changed for the worst. People beefing and downing each other. Satan doesn't hold you up with temptations of doing drugs, drinking, and lust, these things greet you as soon as you get home from prison, every which way you turn. The battle for your soul is a never ending one.

I stayed on the positive road for about a month. When everybody is used to you being out, spending money on you, and showing some form of love, then the point of reality hits, as far as how you're going to make money, are you gonna stay away from the things that can land you back to prison. These decisions control the very road you've allowed yourself to go down. As for me, I chose hanging out, doing what people in the hood call try to play catch up, which means doing what everybody else is doing, getting drunk, smoking weed, and liking the attention that people with a lot of money get. Basically, all the wrong shit.

Same Ole, Same Ole

CHAPTER 15

Like a lot of people forced to come back around the same environment that got them sent to prison isn't an excuse, but rather a harsh, temptation driven war to be in, and if you're not mentally strong, and find new avenues to venture, you'll find yourself in Deja Vu all over again. Instead of moving forward, I allowed myself to eventually yearn for every negative thing I should have run from. I didn't search for a job and eventually found myself needing money and nothing worse than getting out of prison and don't got a dime. like every other ghetto person would do, I did also, went to my friends who could help my problems, (drug dealers), and I started selling weed in the apartments (the villa) I grew up in. Money was coming in good, but I found myself stagnated by waking up doing the same ole things, day and night, drinking, smoking weed, and packing guns. My big home Mike Holland's was throwing a BBQ, and told me to come through. Our homeboy Boomer was going to be there, and he wanted me to chill with him, cause I rapped, and our homeboy was producing an album coming out soon called "Alien Planet". I rapped for him and he said he wanted me to do a song with our homeboy Randy Savage called "Victim to The System". We got to know each other and eventually did the song, which ended up being a nice little hit for the album.

Boomer became a big brother to figure to me. He owned a car wash that we would be allowed to work or chill out at, and it kept me out of trouble. Everybody in Beecher loved the fact that we might be blowing up in the music business, and my hood gave us a lot of support and love. One day my homie

Lil Twan found out I was out, and we rode around drinking all that day, and he told me he wanted me to go with him later that night to pick his girl up in Flushing.

All that day Twan was speeding in this little car that went like 130mph, sounds turned up, and we were highly intoxicated. Knowing we were over our limits we still carried on, knowing we shouldn't have been even thinking about driving on the highway. We still planned too, not knowing what fate had in store for that night. The only thing that stopped me from jumping on the highway with Twan was by us picking up another one of our homeboys that I don't know till this day why Twan picked him up even though they were beefing, (God intervened), no sooner than it was time to get on the highway, Twan and our homeboy Archie went from arguing to the point we got to the store, they jumped out and started fighting. Our

homeboy Archie got the best of him, and Twan
jumped in the car and left us both at the store.

I woke up the next morning to everybody looking at
me like a ghost cause everybody in the Villa Projects
who seen us last, knew I was suppose to go to Flushing
with Twan, and come to find out Twan jumped on
the highway, drunk and speeding, hit the wall on the
highway and was thrown from the car and instantly
killed, my heart stopped, I couldn't believe what I was
hearing, I couldn't believe how something so strange
as Twan picking up Archie on his own while they had
been into it, and the fact that through Archie, God got
me out the car minutes before getting on the highway.
Like so many other times, I still was running around
blinded to what was really going on spiritually, and
how God intervenes in
our lives.

God Testing My Faith

CHAPTER 16

I finished parole with the blessing of The Most High, and was still doing my music thing, I had a relationship with my soon to be second mother of my child Shenina. We had an apartment, her, and her two sons, Deonta, and Tyquan. Everything was going good with us, it's just that I couldn't keep myself from hanging on the streets. Between the music and hanging on the streets, it began to create problems in our relationship. Like in any relationship, time is valuable, and can come back to haunt you if you're not careful. Not only was I hanging out, I began going on dope runs out of town with a homeboy of mine, even though it wasn't for my benefit, I liked to go anyway, do to being around someone making money. We drove to other places in Michigan handling business, even though I didn't sell drugs, I went just to watch my homeboy back. It's like every time I got ready to go she would say things like something bad is going to end up happening. women have a special gift from God, we call it women's intuition, a spiritual instinct to know when bad things are coming, or about bad people.

She would tell me to stay for our family's sake, meaning my oldest daughter Andreada, my two stepsons, my newborn Takoya, and my daughter Geneva, whom she was pregnant with. God talking through her, I still ignored the signs and told her I will be back from Detroit and home soon. I jumped in the car not knowing this would be the reason I was gonna be taken away from my family or see my unborn for 3 and a half years. We got to Detroit, and everything went as usual, we'd hang out, drink a little, wait for the call, pick it up, and head back. We got back to Flint a little late, so he wanted to make a few moves before taking me home, not knowing the State Police was at the end of the street with their lights off watching his spot. Soon we left and turned the corner, you could see the red lights shining on top. He instantly started flying through the stop signs with them being so close on us. I helped him throw the bag when I jumped out of the car running. Thinking that it was only one cop he hit the brakes, I jumped out and took off running.

To my amazement, it happened to be two of them, so when I jumped out, his partner jumped out also chasing behind me. I stopped to throw it over in a yard some dudes were in, I was hoping they'd start grabbing the dope, but while throwing it, the officer grabbed me, and we began to tussle. While tussling with the officer to get free and run, the officer took whatever abuse I gave, just to hold on to me until help came, which wasn't long.

Help arrived, and they apprehended me. They took us both down to the Michigan State Police Precinct for further questioning and check the dope they found. What was so simple, end up being a thorn in my back. All they said was we know that your friend is a well-known drug dealer, we've been watching him, and we seen him give you the paper bag when you jump out.

I denied what they said so we both were taken to the county jail to be arraigned for the same drugs cause they said they seen him give the bag to me. We were arraigned and given bonds. Him having money, he got out right away, leaving me still in there. While in there, the narcotics officers paid me a visit, hoping I would rat my homeboy out, but I denied everything. They did what all police try to do, and they scare you with threats, which didn't work either. I remained in jail for about a week and a half, and my homeboy got me out on Bond. Happy to be free and be with my family, but I still knew I had some tough tribulations ahead of me, for something that I allowed myself to be put in. In the beginning, we were arraigned together, but with him having a paid lawyer, his lawyer eventually got our case separated somehow without me even going to court yet. Which meant that with the drugs being found in my possession, and not in the car, that he was free from the charges, and I was stuck being charged with drugs everybody knew wasn't mine.

I finally got to visit my attorney, which happened to be a court appointed lawyer. He told me while I was still locked up, he'd received a visit from my girlfriend Shenina and come to find out he not only knew, her Aunt Lynn (R.I.P.), and her Grandmother Peggy. Through the blessings of God, he went overboard for me on my case. He started telling me about how he felt about the case, and what he knew about it. He started talking to me to see if I was naive to really what was going on. So, with me not responding, he began speaking bluntly. He asked how do you think he got his charges dropped, I asked how and he told me that the only way a Judge would dismiss a charge that's being charged to two people was if one said he don't know what the other possessed on him when they jumped out the car. I asked him about the police statement on him passing the bag, he stated that that could only be corroborated too, was if I testified to him passing me the bag, other than that it would be stuck as being mine, and my homeboy knew this. Now I was stuck between choosing my family and testifying, or choosing the streets, and taking the charge for a homeboy who obviously didn't give a damn about my life worth or my family losing me. This created a whole lot of chaos in my relationship, due to my pregnant girlfriend breaking down from the thoughts of losing me to me taking the charges for my homeboy, and a lot of people in the hood felt the same way.

Not picturing myself on the stand pointing the finger, I took the charges and like most people in the hood, I chose the streets and took the charge pleading guilty and got sentenced to 3 and a half years in prison, taken away from my young family and away from my unborn child. God gave me a choice, and I chose wrong over right. I failed God's test and paid a big price for it and was sent back to prison.

Back To Prison

CHAPTER 17

Being sent back to prison is a form of stupidity that will ride your back, day and night when you're put back in there, cause leaving prison, you tell yourself I ain't never coming back and your own conscious makes sure your mind replays that thought over and over again. The only thing different was I wasn't the same young stupid 17 year old. This time I was a 27 year old fool. Even though I was very angry about being back, if felt different to me for some reason, and that reason was due to me knowing that I wasn't in here for being the wild young child I was ten years ago, now I was in here for a decision I should of known not to involve myself in. I had to deal with the consequences like any adult who'd made a wrong choice in life. Instead of letting this anger tear me down for 3 and a half years, I started working on my spirituality.

A few months into my prison sentence, I received news that my girlfriend Shenina had our daughter Geneva, this brought a little life back into me to get my mind right mentally, physically, and spiritually. I began getting my read on, and surrounding myself around ones on the same page as me, and told myself that this was going to be one of the biggest lessons I could ever learn in life, pure choices of right and wrong.

Signs & Symbols (In People)

CHAPTER 18

When you go to prison, you seem to get a form of intuition of your own, to know things about people when you hear them or see them, but not everybody has learned to use this blessing from The Most High. A lot of people have the same frame of mind while they're still in prison, and it's easy to see these types. The longer you're at a prison, the more familiar you get with the people jailing there, and what traits they have. It seems like after I got sent to prison for someone's else mess, my mind wouldn't let me put myself in that type of situation no more. I started really dealing with people off of instinct, and not just to be doing something. I didn't wanna sit and talk about garbage not worth talking about. I seemed to be tired of being around people like this. God gave me a gift that I'd begin to read people intuitively, just like my mother, and the other of my children, and lots of people I knew had. They'd say something ain't right about this or that person, or don't go there, something might end up happening, and just like them, my own intuitions were beginning to show me things, and the results began to amaze me.

Mental Awakening

———— ❦ ————

CHAPTER 19

My second time in prison, me and my conscious was my biggest enemy at this time. I couldn't really be mad at my homeboy, cause at the end of the day, I didn't have to except the bag, or jump out the car, so solely alone, I did this to myself. For the first time in my life I started planning on a way of life to avoid the very hell I grew in, and allowed myself to become a better person inside out. Religion could help, but a person has to come to the understanding of wanting to become his religion, and not just have one. I started really aiming towards disciplining self along with spirituality in order to keep myself spiritually awoke, mentally and physically.

Racial Difference

CHAPTER 20

One of the other differences I found myself needing to work on was hatred that a lot of people don't even know they have. What I mean they don't know they have is a lot of people are racist, and don't even know it. You got many ways a person can be, or become racist, rather racist in any form or fashion is still racist. Some people will be quick to blame it on their upbringing, meaning their parents and other relatives were racist, so it passed on to them, which can only come about if you're too scared to stand up for yourself and say you feel differently than they do. While some had things happen to them, or people in their same race, like being lynched, jumped on, called names, bad relationships, stereotypes, or just being plain ole different.

On the streets, black people are considered the minority, due to it being more white people in America than blacks, but in Michigan, black inmates, along with Hispanics, run the penitentiary. This sudden trading of places, blacks and Hispanics seem to get some get back for the racial tension they've encountered from in a racist country that pretends not to be, me included. I had racial tension already in me before I went to prison, like from racist police in my community, teachers not from our community, unwelcome behavior coming from whites, when we were in their communities.

I never gave myself a chance to see it any different than I felt already. This created a lot of problems while in prison cause I never really gave it a chance to really get to know people cause they were white, but the more I started studying self, without letting others dictate how and what I thought. I started learning to judge people on their own personal characteristics, and not cause the color of people skin. Which is backward thinking, cause no matter what color a person is, you've still got crazy, shady people of every race. When I was able to purify myself of this, I could feel myself getting more humble, more self aware, more spiritual inside and outward towards people. I was really working towards my higher self, and I learned to deal with people according to their personal behavior, and not race they were, which made it better for me dealing with life and people.

New Energy Spiritually

CHAPTER 21

When beginning to work on yourself, you start to see different angles from which Satan tries to attack you. Everybody doesn't get attacked in the same form or fashion. Just like with God's way of working with each person in different unique way, so does Satan. Unlike God, Satan waits for a chance to influence you off of your own anger, jealousy, lust, or any other things that bring you down to a lower state away from God. Also, when you are on the road to a higher self he distracts you to try and make you jump off your road to higher self. Me working on my higher self, and feeling good within about it, I'd just had a newborn child and a family waiting on me, here comes Satan.

One night in a dream, I had a dream of the mother of my children Shenina being pregnant, so I wrote a letter to her telling her my dream I had. She responded to me saying I was tripping, and that it couldn't possibly be true cause she wasn't doing anything. as the months went by, my own intuitions started giving me signals from how she'd word things in letters off of what say to her, eventually she sent me a picture displaying the bulge in her stomach, she replied that she was pregnant, and by whom. It hurt more cause it was by a brother I grew up with in the hood, but I couldn't be angry with her for going on with her life, due to me getting myself locked up. I could not believe the vision was true and God showed me and not only that, the friend who betrayed me ended up at the same prison I was. We ended up talking about it and I couldn't decide what I wanted to do about it, or how it really affected me, but the night he packed up to go to another prison. I cracked his head with a master combination lock in a sock, due to the fact I wasn't over the pain of it all, even though I was angry with her. I still came to the understanding that I'd been gone for 3 years and I had to decide if I could accept these things like she did when I messed up (God's test), but the only difference was she wasn't locked up when I was with other women and could I force her to stop her life just cause I've gotten locked up.

I talked to my spiritual brothers in prison with me, as well as my mother on the phone, who made me come to the conclusion that if I really loved her, I would have a big responsibility spiritually to make it workout without judging or downing her. We dealt with it together on the phone and through letters, trying to move forward together and make it work. To me, it not only showed spiritual growth, but it also that you never really knew how it felt for God to forgive us, until we have learned to forgive others. God opened my eyes once more and before I knew it was time to go home again, after 3 and half years.

Released to a Chaotic World for the Second Time

CHAPTER 22

Since being paroled the second time around, I was happy physically, but on the inside, I felt kinda scared cause I really didn't know how I would really feel being put in a situation of meeting my daughter Geneva for the first time, and my step daughter Ashawnta. I had butterflies in my stomach the whole ride home. Once I arrived, I hugged everyone, and introduced myself to Ashawnta and let nature take its course. Her being two years old, she stayed under me just like the rest of the children, and before you knew it, we were back a happy family, with two new members of the tribe, Geneva and Ashawnta.

The blessings kept coming, my uncle Haywood visited me; to tell me he had a house open for me and my family to move in, so we did. It was a whole new beginning for all of us. I had a meeting with a local rap label, who wanted me to be on their label, I made a song called (Bang Dis), which was bound to be a local hit in Flint, but the more I hung around the studio, the more I saw that they were into more than music. It would be times were while we were in the studio, they had a lot more hot, messy type shit going on, from dope to drama on the street, beef with other hoods and then with my crew being with me from Beecher (Vice Lords and Bloods), and the fact I didn't really know these cats.

Even though I was used to being around environments like this, I felt God was telling me to remember what I've just gotten out of prison for, which was for someone's else mess, meaning get caught up in their bullshit. Also, the fact that I'm on parole, and ain't supposed even be around this type of stuff. This left everybody wondering why I was running from a for sure record deal. When I was really staying away to save my freedom (I listened to God), which led me and the crew to part. I continued to focus on positivity and finished parole, and my girlfriend Shenina was pregnant with Teron Jr. after! She gave birth to Teron Jr., and it gave me a real reason to sit still and focus on our family.

I stayed from hanging out on the streets a lot, cause I already knew what that would have me into, and before you know it, your actions allow a way for evil to interfere (Satan), in your lives. While everything was going good under the God's grace, the only mistake I made was not going out and getting a job, and tryna earn a legit living. Before long, money became a big issue that would drive you insane mentally and physically. Living in a poverty stricken environment, led me to thinking of all types of different crimes, instead of just getting a job.

Wanting the easy life haunted me daily, rap music wasn't moving fast enough. I started selling crack cocaine. This got me money really quick and before you knew it, I was addicted to the fast money and didn't wanna do nothing else. Stuck in a zone of greed cause it comes so easily off other people's addictions, and even though it's wrong, people accept it due to the greed of money.

My girlfriend She didn't condone it either, but still was amazed at the wealth it produced. Meaning she accepted the money, but disagreed with the risk, and didn't allow it to be sold around our home. People might think that money buys happiness, it doesn't. The more money I began making illegally, it seems the farther down the wrong road I began going. My girlfriend Shenina didn't like the road I was on either, cause the more money, the later I stayed out, the more I would party, which led to me constantly being around and messing around with other women. In the midst of this chaos, I started using my money to create my own rap group and pay for studio time.

Eventually Shenina had enough of me not being home, not giving her the love she deserved, and she found it elsewhere, and bout time the end of the road came for both of us, the split was full of resentment and anger, with the children suffering most. At that time, I had another baby on the way by the third mother of my children Kristen. This gave me a full run down a bad road, partying and nothing to balance any good in me, and around me. My whole day revolved around me selling drugs, doing music, drinking, and overnight parties with different women. It seems like even though I was doing wrong, I could feel that The Most High had his grips on me cause I had a lot of good intentions, but was just making a lot of bad decisions.

Rap seemed to be the only thing keeping me from being fully on negative things, even though it brought a lot of things around me. My homeboy lil Phil and some of his relatives and homies I knew, started a rap group called the Da FAM, which consisted of me, lil Phil (R.I.P.), Noodles, J Dubb, Willie Bam, D.P mighty dollas (R.I.P.), Lil Muscle and M.G., all we did was eat, sleep, drink, smoke weed, sell drugs, and party. Around this time Kristen had my son Treyshawn. Kristen tried to make it work, but just like my other relationships, I wasn't doing the right things, and Kristen didn't agree with my lifestyle, and eventually left me to do the things I had gotten accustomed to doing.

The more shows and music we did, the more partying and selling drugs we did. Just like anywhere else, the more problems on the streets we started having. Some of the group ended up having beef with another group from our neighborhood in Beecher, called F.O.E., who some of our members had personal problems with, which led to beefing on music, to beefing on sight. Just like in any hood beefing leads to fights, gunplay, which leads to buying guns, and carrying guns. Which we did and kept around us day and night. It got so bad that police started getting involved, and called themselves shutting us all down, to the point they knew us all by name, and found out about the dope I was pushing, and the amount of heat we had. Any time they got the chance they would raid, or run up in any spot hey got the word we was at.

Constant failures at trying to catch us in the wrong they knew us to be doing, we ended up taking over a mini apartment complex called (the bricks). We had an apartment at the top floor with a stripper our rap member Kay had met. Us taking over these apartments made the Beecher police put us on they number one get list. Even though we were doing a lot of wrong, we escaped a lot of that wrong by people covering for us, cause we showed a lot of love to the people in my hood, and a lot of them times I would thank God, and let the rest of the group know that I felt we were escaping a lot of this wrong, due to the good things we were doing. For example, taking care of each other's families, housing for each other, food, and looking out for people's families, neighbors and more and at the same time trying to go legit through making music. I think God knew what our true intentions were, even though we were doing wrong to be able to do it.

The Third Eye

CHAPTER 23

It took a long time for me to understand people that say God helped, or saved them, especially when their doing wrong. Now I've seen a lot in my life. From good and bad, angelic to demonic, and physical and spiritual. Although we were steadily running around doing bad, I didn't forget the spiritual side that God showed me. Everyone around me, loved me, cause I had this gift to bring spiritual effects on people, even while selling drugs I still had it in me not to mislead people away from God. I did not force anyone to accept the bad things I was doing, by trying to pass it off as good. I loved helping and assisting people at times, it came back to me, meaning, a lot of people reciprocated that same love for me, in times of need and I thank God they did. I earned money the wrong way, it still felt good inside, being able to help those in need who I knew really needed it.

I was aiming at a righteous life, but falling short of it chasing money illegally. I started using my third eye, which is nothing more than a connection cord to The Most High, while were in the flesh. Many doors are open through this gate, but only you and God know what he's allowed you to know and see through your third eye. I met my fourth baby mother Nicole, and as we got more involved, I had a vision in my dream of her being pregnant, and with this being the second time I had a vision like this, I awoke and told her, and she laughed it off, but eventually snuck and got a test and found out she was. This wouldn't be the last vision I had come true.

Technological Mind Control

———— ⚬❦⚬ ————

CHAPTER 24

Having my six children on the way by Nicole, we spent a lot more time together. However, I spent most of the time with my kids, my music, selling dope and partying. At this time technology was beginning to get really advanced, from phones to laptops, computers, and the internet, which meant people were connecting from all over the United States of America, which meant everything started speeding up. Along with this high-tech technology, came a price, and that price was selfishness, family disunity, and everybody being turned on to the good and the bad that this world has to offer at a push of a button. MySpace had everybody online 24 hours a day, as if under a spell. Many people stayed glued to the portals on a screen, that seemed to take people out of this world and into another one alone. Satan had arrived through their waves, (lord of the air), to take the natural minds of God's creation. What was once traditional through God, became tainted by Satan's technology, (to erase our spiritual minds).

Spiritual Visions of The Future

The plugs on the music getting better, and technology speeding up people mind, America was on a historical pace itself, a black man by the name Barack Obama was on the verge of becoming President of the United States. We were doing good making moves on our music career, when my homeboy Kay baby mother introduced me to Deanna, who would end up being my fifth baby mother. We met and come to find out her homegirl Em Dawg was a music engineer. We all got acquainted quickly. We started messing around and they started coming down to Flint. The rap group I was in would go up there to their city, and we would party. With me hustling, and having a baby on the way, I'd stay down in Flint most the time with Nicole.

One morning I was laying down with Nicole, and I received a call from the members of my rap group who said they were on they to get me, to bring me up there, so we could rob this dude for some thousands by acting like we had some pounds of weed. We get up there to pick the dude up to take us where the money was. We got to some apartments, with dudes standing around like they were guarding the apartments. The dude jumped out to go get the money, so I got out and went to the trunk to grab a bag to act like it's weed in it and jumped back in the car.

Em Dawg and G start getting nervous cause of all the dudes standing around, and it was only one way out of these apartments, and it would be a gamble to risk pulling out and them shooting the car up, but we did it anyway. The dude jumped back in the car and I put the gun to his rib and told Em Dawg to start driving. The dudes started walking up, and I told him to tell hold up, as if we'd be right back, and we creeper up out of there.

We got like six blocks down the road and seen a car following us. We stopped at the red light, and seen some one jump out a car. I put the guy out the back seat, so I could see who running up on our car. I put the gun towards the window, ready to shoot, till I seen that it was Lil Muscle and J Dubbed, who happen to follow us to make sure we was straight. We went back to Dee and Em Dawg spot to grab what they could cause we rob knew where they stayed.

They decided to move to Flint, we all end up going in on a house to put our studio in to begin making our songs. Obama was running for president, we made a song called it's time for a change, that we begin passing out during the election. Election night we celebrated a future event so many black people visioned and prayed tone alive to see (a blackman became President of the United States of America). Around that same time we found out Deanna was pregnant.

Satan's Earthly Kingdom

CHAPTER 26

I name this chapter, Satan's earthly kingdoms cause, whenever you create a paradise for bad reasons, you can just about depict what's gonna come about out of this. Now money from the robbery got us the house, and nobody had in their mind making it a real spot, but me, Dee and Em Dawg, cause everybody else was just there leeching off my money, and a place to stay. We partied like rock stars, sold dope out of it, and did our music, day in and day out. Now the first month there, a shoot out happened on the otherwise of the hood in Beecher, and some members of DA FAM were said to have been there. We received a call about it, giving us a heads up, that the police were coming. The next thing you know, 4 different counties of police pulled up, guns out, telling everyone inside to come out with our hands up.

They searched the house and found nothing linking us to the shooting, so they left. Everyday it seemed to be different drama in the crib. Members of the rap group getting drunk and fighting, different women in and out, getting into it about members of the group. Police were on me cause they got word I was posted in there. They started watching the spot and then Nicole found out Deanna was staying there, she came over acting a fool, to the point where Deanna yelled out to her that she was pregnant too, and they were at each other verbally every time they crossed paths.

I was happy about my babies being on the way, but mad about the drama it created between them. This house was purchased of something evil and that's how it destroyed itself. A little after that, Lil Red took his soon to be baby's mother to the hospital, cause she felt it was time to have the baby, while they were gone. Me and Dee had gone back to sleep, and I had a dream of a pale shaped face with a upside down frown on it. I woke up and told Dee about it, and later that morning, we received a text message picture of Lil Red still born baby having the same facial look as my dream. It blew our minds. Bad things continued happening until Deanna had enough and left me. I ended up moving in with Nicole, and the rap group spread out also. The house was left abandoned. Environments like this give Satan a chance to keep chaos going.

Demonic Behavior

CHAPTER 27

I moved in with Nicole it felt strange cause it had been a while since I'd been in a family structured home! Meaning the wild things, I was doing the past two and a half years. It's like for two and a half years, I was able to run around, with no responsibilities, partying, selling drugs, drinking, robbing, and sleeping with all types of different women. Keeping guns on me at all times. When we got to our house, it was like coming out of a hellish zone, and now I was in complete silence. Then it seemed different when people came through and wanted it to be like it used to be, meaning party, sleepovers, full of people who were only there for what benefitted them, which was free drinks, drugs and somewhere to sleep. To me it started appearing like evil was lurking tempting people to do bad stuff.

Demonic forces trying to leech their way in through individual people, in order to keep me in a behavioral pattern of doing wrong, or effect my surroundings, and in this way effect my very life. A few months of being in our new home, Nicole gave birth to my newborn baby girl Nikiyah, so this gave me a lease on how I move. Just like always, when things start to get right, Satan be waiting, to make it wrong. Behavior from your past will always test you in the present. It was a never ending plight to try and get me to do the bad things, I was accustomed to doing. If it wasn't people surrounding me with drinks, weed, and women, it would be people getting into it with other people, to pull me in. I tried to stay focused on our music, and my family. Demons are forever around, even in the flesh of people.

The Prophet Job

CHAPTER 28

When you read about the Prophet Job, in the Bible, you come to find out how Satan was given permission to test Job in certain matters. Satan came to a Congregational meeting, stating a claim in front of The Most High. God ask Satan where was he coming from, and Satan replied, from going to and from the on the earth, from walking up and down on it. God spoke highly of Job and that made Satan wanted to test Job in anyway he could but only by how The Most High allowed him too. Satan first started by destroying his property, and herds, killing his servants, to even his family, with hopes Job turning his back to The Most High, and he refused.

After that didn't work, Satan came before The Most High again and The Most High spoke highly of Job again. This time The Most High allowed Satan to cause an illness to befall on Job in hopes that he would curse The Most High, but he still refused, even though his wife and friends, through Satan working through them, in order to tempt him into turning from God.

Every human being is a creation of The Most High and a potential Job, and Satan will try us all in the same manners as he tried Job. When me and Nicole got house together, and she gave birth to Nikiyah, I felt good within, but was constantly being challenged in ways to pull me back into the fast-paced chaotic world I was accustomed to living. We made a studio in our home, but I had refused to let it turn into what the last house turned into, especially with my new born baby, and two stepsons: Travis and Dayshawn being there.

Within a year of Nicole having Nikiyah, she found out

she was pregnant again, another girl, who she'd eventually name Sakara. Life was good at this time, but the only problem was the Beecher Police would not let up on me, or my rap group. One night we had a get together, and the police rolled pass and started harassing everybody in the yard. My home boy Lil Phil gave them the middle finger. The officer stopped, and before I knew it, a whole bunch of police cars stopped and rushed the yard. One of the officers who came was an officer I had a real problem with.

They snatched me up and put me in the police car and this officer drove off with me to the police station, not knowing they had snatched began up my boy Lil Phil too. Soon as we got to the police station, they took me out of the car and this officer began to assault me, stopped, and took me to a holding cell and they began beating me again. After leaving my cell, you could hear him go across to the other holding cell, and they begin assaulting Lil Phil. After they finished assaulting us, they put us back in the car and dropped us off at the gas station down the street. Made my way back home, where the police continued to harass my home.

I eventually got a lawyer and put a lawsuit in just to put some heat on back on them, and they illegal tactics. After the lawsuit was put in, and they saw I wasn't just some uneducated criminal from the streets, they began harassing people coming for studio time, friends of me and Nicole. I started letting them see me take pictures of the on camcorder. A little further down Nicole's pregnancy, I ended up doing some county jail time where the Judge allowed me to turn myself in. We partied with champagnes and liquor mixed, and we went to the county jail in a crewed up car line, so I could turn myself in. During me doing my time, I got out after a couple of months and found out Deanna had my son Dominic, which made my day. Now I had two new kids: Nikiyah and Dominic, and another one on the way by Nicole,

Sakara.. Just like Job, Satan waited for happiness to come to attack.

While I was out for a couple of days from home, I got a call from Nicole saying one of the boys was messing around with candles and the house caught on fire. I hurried home to see the house on fire, but happy to see Nicole and our kids were alright, along with our puppies, but the older dog died. We were able to stay with Momma Lisa and Lil Muscle till we got our other house. It's crazy that the fire happened on Christmas Eve, but we had hidden all the presents in the laundry room, where the fire didn't hit. We received things from people Nicole knew, and some things from my peeps, and my O.G.Chris brown (R.I.P.). Nicole began stressing from which was affecting her late in her pregnancy, due to her not eating cause of stress, with the blessings of The Most High we got another crib before it was time for her to have the baby. After being in the new house for a month, she gave birth to my daughter Samara, the youngest of my tribe.

Spiritual Entities

CHAPTER 29

The Most High was definitely shining on me. New home, a newborn baby, and a big family, I had due to The Most High blessing me with a large family tree. I slowed down from the music and focused more on my family. I slowed down from partying and hanging on the streets but was still selling dope. I started keeping my kids around each other more, so they'd know each other due to me having five baby mothers. It seems like I've always had visions, I've always seen entities.

One morning while me and Nicole got up around sunrise to get the boys ready for school. I happen to look out the window to see light beings by a bush, but not in the bush, levitating like, one row above the other. They appeared to be in a light that was different from the reflection from the sun coming up. Thinking I was tripping, I called Nicole to see if she could see the same thing I did and she did. I told her to describe what she was seeing to make sure she was really seeing it and she was. After all these years, I was seeing entities again but these were peaceful, unlike the ones I saw when I was a child. They left as they came, in peace. They would continue to show me more.

UFO's
(Fiery Chariots)

CHAPTER 30

After seeing the beings of light in the bush, it seemed like I was back checking my surroundings to see what I can see. The first summer at our new house me and Nicole used to sit outside at night and chill. The later at night it got, we would see what appeared to be UFO's, way up in the sky. As time passed each night, it seems like it was getting closer and closer, but never close enough to see actually what it was. One night we was up real late, and I was smoking a cigarette in the kitchen, while Nicole was in the living room watching

T.V., talking to me back and forth. I turned to talk towards the room she was in and when I turned back towards the open window. I saw the large aircraft that was the size of a house in between our house, and the neighbors, but didn't hit none of the trees or bushes in between these two houses. As if it was going through them. I ran towards the living room yelling to Nicole to come see. Soon as we got outside, we could see the beautiful orange craft that seemed to be moving noiseless, and at a speed unbelievable, and turned down a street two blocks down at a 180 degree turn, moving like a ghost. Me and Nicole couldn't believe our eyes. I've never seen anything this color and shape in my life.

The second craft we seen was the triangle shape UFO, we were in the back of the house, and on the other side of the hood, we seen a craft come straight up to the sky, and start flying, soon as I pointed the way it went, the craft turned and came towards where we were at, as if it seen me pointing. It came over our home making no noise like the other craft, about 200 feet above our home, an all black triangle, with three white light at each point, and a red light in the middle. In shock, I kept looking and Nicole panicked and said she was gonna go check on the kids cause she was scared. She ran to the back stairs to the back of the house and as if we were in a hypnotic state. The lights on the craft appeared to blink from low, back to bright and it took off slowly and quietly. I looked and Nicole was still on the stairs, and I was still in the same spot, but it was almost time for daybreak, which should have been impossible. Me and Nicole had witnessed both a physical craft (the triangle), to a ghostly craft (big orange craft), up close and personal. Who's in them, or where they come is unknown, but they are here, and they are real and it makes you think about the fiery chariots spoken of in the Bible.

Bibles Banned

It is hard to believe that a world could be controlled by spiritual evil. Or is it people don't really believe in the scriptures like they say they do. This world is turning more evil by the day, by the month, by the year. People claim the world is getting better through technology, but are we really getting better. Who is controlling such actions that would make a God fearing nation allow anyone to ban Holy Scriptures. The first thing a person will say is it's due to respect to other religions, but if that's the case, why not still recognize the oneness of The Most High, One Brotherhood. America being a Bible based nation, it seems a little crazy to take God out of the minds of the people, whereas other Countries lead their nation off of their religions. Christianity, Islam, Buddhism, and Judaism, etc...

Anytime you take God away from the minds of the people, especially in places we are teaching children, who are learning how to develop themselves, you're allowing them to look at the world from a nonspiritual view. At which their views are left for them to pick and choose from a savage, man-made view of life. When you look at the early '50s and '60s, people kept God mentioned in conversation. Schools National Anthem, by neighbors etc... From the 70's to the present, it's been an attack against God, allowed by the leaders of the country, who are putting science and technology in and the mention of God out. Now you've got generations of people growing up without the knowledge of God, or the Bible. Then they wonder why the world is becoming a Godless acting world. Bibles being banned should be a message, that Satan has control of the world, and by taking God out of the minds of the people, and putting Satanic propaganda in, God is gonna bring America (New Babylon), to its knees.

Spiritual Death
Around The World

CHAPTER 32

Sometimes I ask myself, how is it that the world we live in remains as barbaric as it is today. People starving still, killing each other constantly. War everywhere, world leaders promising one thing, and doing another. It seems like spiritually, we are not only moving backwards instead of forward, but nobody seems to care. America for example, use to be in the front line of good faith and spirituality. When some of the founding fathers made the Declaration of Independence, they made sure that God's laws, not man, came first and for the people. This assured people that under God's law, that things would remain

MY ROAD TO THE MOST HIGH   111

for the people, and therefore would never change. This ideology made America prosper in ways never seen before around the world. Not only spiritually, but physically. Becoming the front runner of a world in development, dreams and ideals become manifest, but also in showing the world that by coming together, that any and all goals can come to fruition. It seems like the world stop caring about others, and just lovers of their own country, or self, therefore allowing leaders to go from using Gods law, to man-made laws of the rich, just like the founding fathers warned us about.

This effect has been passed on to the people, who only care about material, wealth, and nothing more. Now you have a world looking down on countries and people, due to them having lack of money and food. Everything moving so fast, technology, spiritually, we are deteriorating generation by generation. And if we don't regain are spiritual strength under submitting to God, we are doomed for the prophecies mentioned in the scriptures that people are failing to study, or believe.

Mentally Sleep

———— ❧ ————

C H A P T E R   3 3

The ups and downs of my life came, it seemed as if
me, along with the rest of the world, in different forms
and fashions, seem to be stuck in a matrix. Meaning
mentally sleep in some way. Propaganda seemed to
control what we eat, buy, drink, drive, wear, live,
except, etc... Mines was being not able to see what in
my life was pulling me down, over and over again.
Trusting people who didn't deserve to be trusted.
Places I shouldn't have been and chasing dreams that
shouldn't have been chased. Constantly bumping my
head, I began waking up out of my mental sleep and
constant let downs, I was asleep also.

It is on all of us all individually to find what we are mentally asleep to. Please, pray to God to open our eyes to what we see but don't see spiritually, cause sometimes people are rocked to sleep by Satan and get led into a way of life that appears to be good and enticing, just like in the Garden of Eden, with Adam and Eve.

Love & Trust Gone

CHAPTER 34

After my daughter Sakara was born, we were already
in our new house and I'd begun seeing things again.
The whole year was a brand-new start for my whole
tribe, meaning me, Nicole and all our children being
together on the regular. I stopped doing my music and
started allowing all my children to be with me
constantly. The feelings it gave me to see them all
together from different places, brought me a good
feeling, that could come only from The Most High
himself, and I could feel it. Like they say when
things get too good, the bad is always somewhere
waiting. It's that no matter how good a person's heart
is to others, it still doesn't mean the people you
look out for are gonna have the same heart and

feelings that you do, another lesson I had to learn. When I sold drugs, I found myself surrounded by people I assumed had the same love for me. I showed and gave to the ones around me. When you got money, you don't know if people be around you out of love, or just for what they want out of you.

When things get rough for you, you can start to see who is real, and who could care less. I stopped messing with the crowd I was messing with while doing the music, cause to me it didn't seem like real love, and it wasn't. I started hanging back with just my homies I grew up with cause I knew they had a love for me while I had money and way before that and they never changed on me. I was still pushing dope, and the police were still on personally due to me having a lawsuit on them for kidnapping me and assaulting me and my homeboy. That year all types of badness started floating in the atmosphere. My second child mother Shenina, Auntie Lynn, whom I was close with, was killed in car accident.

After that Nicole's mother Tracy, passed away from drinking too much. Me and my brother went to Texas to visit my mother for the first time in years, just to come back to Flint, to hear Curtis was shot down and killed. I watched Curtis grow up, he started doing music with us, and he was really close to me. It hurt bad to hear something like that happen to such an innocent, young talented young brother gets killed for nothing. After burying Curtis, it seemed like fuel continued to be thrown on the fire of life. After all these years, the police finally found someone close to me, who helped them get a very much needed reason to raid my house for drugs. The whole day was kind of slow and crazy, cause I reloaded, meaning bought some more drugs. Some homies who were scared to come to my spot, due to me being watched by the police a lot (first sign), so we met out in the open. Then we got a visit by JDubb and his girl. We sent them to go get some weed from one of the homies in the hood, (second sign). After they came back, we smoked a blunt, and I sat in my favorite lazy boy chair, facing the street. I could see a line of cars coming from both directions, at a fast pace. I yelled to Nicole, to let her know we were getting raided, we ran and got rid of the work we had.

By the time we got back to the living room, police bust the door open with the battle ram and rushed the crib. They entered the house, these police had smiles on their face due to finally being able to raid a house they thought I lived. Using their textbook tactics they went straight after the women first. To no avail, they began threatening me, I told them to do their job. One of the officers came out laughing, when he found some white powder in a plastic bag. I started laughing with him, and he asked me what's so funny, I said cause what you're holding is some residue from some powdered doughnuts. After testing it, you could see the rage on their faces, then they began tearing the ceiling down, pouring bleach on our clothing, cutting cords on appliances, and calling CPS on Nicole.

After searching the house thoroughly, they found a 12 gauge pump and a pistol in a bag of clothes. Satisfied they'd found something. The police let our friends go, and automatically put the gun on me, and took me to the County Jail, knowing by law they couldn't put the guns on me, they P.F.I. (pending further investigation) the guns, and sent me Lapsed for child support. While in Lapeer, my family moved in with my brother Howard, do to fear of retaliation from the police. So, we got out of Beecher and moved to the west side of Flint. I name this chapter Love and Trust gone, to loosing loved ones and me no longer trusting people, like I used to, facts!

2012

———— ❧ ————

CHAPTER 35

Sitting in the county jail again, I not only was gonna miss the holidays with my family. The end of the next year was marking an event that was said to be gonna end life on Earth, as we know it. First, it started with people quoting the Mayan Calendar, which was wrongly quoted as saying its going to be the end of the world. This being said, made the religious groups, and conspiracy theorist, give their opinion on the subject. The real facts coming from the religious point is God says no one knows the day, or the hour, except Him. From the chief elders of learned Mayans, who say this event is not the end of the world, but an upgrade in one's very spiritual being. Meaning God would upgrade one's spirituality, if chosen, or given the chance to raise ourselves to a higher dimension. This was the true meaning of the Mayan Calendar, and 2012.

2012 Spiritual Upgrade Vision

CHAPTER 36

I sat in the county jail while 2012 kicked in, but a little after New Years. I was locked down for night, and fell into a deep sleep, but while being asleep, it's like I had a full awareness of what was going on. Suddenly, I was in the apartments I grew up in, with three guys that I had never seen in my life and all of a sudden a UFO comes out of the clouds and stops midair, about 200ft. above the apartments. It looked like a dumbbell weight, with a circle on both ends, with a bar type shape connecting the circles. We looked at the craft, a bright flash sparked, and all of a sudden, I was aboard what appeared to be a cloud looking room, all white, but without any shapes, or forms in it, and a bright white that I've never seen before. It seems as if I could physically see from a variety of view points. I could see out my eyes and a view above the whole room. It seems as if I could not move from where I was at, or talk out my mouth, all I could hear was a voice in my head from a being talking to me telepathically, standing behind something cloud like. What he was behind had no form, but it looked like everything else in there (cloud like).

The only reason knew it was there was cause it covered the bottom half of the being, from the waist on down. The being looked bright white, with long white hair, and a long white beard. When I say white, I mean a blinding bright white. He never moved from his position, and neither did I. but it appeared to me like I was getting something downloaded in my mind. The only words I could remember telepathically were, you're special, and another flash appeared, and I was back on the ground, in the apartments again, looking at the craft zoom off, and the vision was over, and I woke up. I wrote my Nicole and told Her my vision, knowing she'd believe me do to her seeing the things we'd encountered together, and the things I told her I had seen as a child.

God Upgraded My Abilities

Having that mind blowing vision, I was eventually released out of jail, and back with my family. Now I've always studied subjects concerning the occult, and the people in them who were in high positions, like the armed forces, judges, lawyers, politicians, music producers, movie producers, and book authors, who under occulted teachings, are taught to communicate in signs and numbers. After having my vision, I suddenly noticed an extra ability that I never had before. Some people tell you after having a Godlike spiritual encounter, that they eventually end up having some form of wisdom. Mine wasn't some super like power or anything, but it was an ability to see things like occultist witch craft in signs, and numbers in movies, commercials, T.V shows, food packages, clothing, shoes, and famous people, or politicians hand signals.

This was an ability I've never had or paid any attention to before. It's as if God opened my eyes to be able to see people who under the guidance of Satan, utilized by the mark of the beast talked about in revelations. Come to see that when they say mark of the beast, I learned that these marks are on everything distributed to us from large corporations, marks like the devil's horns, and the numbers 666, 23, 13, 11, 9, 911, and18. All these numbers are found on something given, or showed to us in our everyday lives. Letting you know Satan is real and people are pledging allegiance to him. God Almighty opened my eyes spiritually to these hidden messages, which was truly a blessing from God to see Satan's hidden signs.

T.V
(Satanic Propaganda)

CHAPTER 38

I started to understand more about these signs and symbols and numbers. It made me look at T.V. in a whole new way. It's like I could see and understand how Satan was sneaking his way into all our lives, by using T.V. in the early stages of people getting T.V.'s, you could slowly but surely see that it was getting more away from God, and more evil and Satanic. It used to be a time when if something on the television was too derogatory, people would boycott, and protest, and basically keep people controlling these shows in check on subjects that weren't suitable for underage children, to slowly easing these ungodly agendas on T.V. generation by generation. Shows making heroes out of people standing up for subjects, such as homosexuality, transgender, DNA splicing between humans and animals. Alien DNA enhancing humans, making super soldiers. Cartoons depicting animals talking, lusting for humans and children. Perverted characters lusting for children, witches becoming heroes using demonic powers. To eventually everything on T.V.is full of subjects that go against God and the Holy Scriptures. Years of this propaganda, the next generations get accustomed to it, and accept it as the norm.

 Everything unexceptionable in the Holy Book, is what TV is full of today, and it's getting worse and worse. What a better way for Satan to expose people to the evils of the unseen world than with T.V.

The Internet

C H A P T E R 3 9

T.V. is one of Satan's many tools, but the internet has the minds of everyone in one fashion or another. Social media, Facebook, Twitter, YouTube, and FaceTime, are just a few of the Internet's Satanic weapons. Don't get me wrong, good things can come from using the internet also. The thing is, the availability of good and bad, perversion, lust, self-idolization at the push of a button is a lot on the table for a young mind to indulge in or make a decision on. The faster the technology, the easier it is for young inexperienced minds to venture off into without guidance from a mature adult. Anytime children can get excess to pornography and weapons creating, people killing and fighting each other.

Seeing boys and girls, who wanna change their gender, or be preyed upon by the same sex, due to being vulnerable from let downs from the opposite sex. A lot of these subjects are not only ungodly but are subjects that a person should be able to deal with as an adult, and not as a child. People have gotten so caught up in technology, that they feel out of place to oversee the things that their children are tuning into. But the people creating these websites have a responsibility also, to screen what ages people have to be to get on these websites, and ownership of the person who name the phone is under. Meaning if the people whose names are given as the owner of the phone is underage, certain websites should be unavailable to underage people. If parents' names are on them, they should already have sanctions put on internet access from certain websites. Us as parents have to take back control on what our kids are tuned into and learning without us being there to guide them. Innocent children shouldn't have access to the evils of the world, and able to make adult decisions, as a child.

Are Keypads On Appliances Ouija Boards

CHAPTER 40

If you've ever seen an ouija board, in real life, or t.v., and looked at the keypads to a computer, laptop, phone, etc... you will see a similarity between them. All of them are designed the same way. You ask a question on an ouija board, that has letters to spell out the words, and you get an answer back from a spirit. They say the board itself is designed to open up a portal once you begin the ritual of communication. The spirit answers questions that are asked by the person opening the portal. Now technology (Satan's creation) has made them digital, to where you type something on the keypads, and a circle starts to spin, as if a portal is being opened, and something answers you back.

Giving a form of wisdom that you've required. Ancient legends talk about how witches used to talk into things they called black mirrors (the screens on a computer, laptop and phones), and spirits would appear showing people things. Remember the wicked witch on the wizard of oz, and the crystal ball. The witch on snow white talking to a black mirror, until a spirit appeared.

What about companies showing you technology with an apple, with a bite taken out it (Adam and Eve with the Apple that gave them knowledge and wisdom of good and bad, (sounds like the internet doesn't it.), or what about I-phones, (the all seeing eye of Satan), which is satellites, cameras on laptops, phones, or anything with cameras using technology to watch our every move, to mock God, who doesn't need technology. Now you've got devices that you can communicate back and forth with (A.I: Artificial Intelligence or spirits) that not only watch you, but also control your other technology around you. This new technology is inviting spirits into our homes, through portals and electric currents in the appliances. Satan's master plan is to get us to indulge in a form of witchcraft, unknowingly, by calling it artificial intelligence.

Being Able To See Evil In The Flesh

CHAPTER 41

After I got out of jail, and we moved on the westside of Flint. I not only had the ability to see the signs, symbols, and numbers. I also started being able to see things in myself, and other people. The things I'm talking about are ways that the evil ones get inside people, you can see when the evil ones get into people. Demons and other evil spirits have to wait to be invited into you unless they fully possess you, and by that I mean when you get angry, you hear whispers in your mind telling you to do things you eventually regret when they leave your mind, that's why most people ask themselves, why did I do that, meaning something influenced your mind and reactions, and then left. Then there's times when people are drinking, and become someone else, while drinking is considered being an alcoholic, but does being considered an alcoholic define why you temporarily become a totally different person while intoxicated on alcohol.

People act differently and have multiple personalities. Some are violent, some cry a lot, some become talkative, but most become another person they don't usually be, and with drugs, it's the same thing, but with drugs it gets a little deeper, cause drugs open up portals to the unseen and other senses we don't have excess to on the regular and invite things in. The main point is that evil enters you and me, when we are angry, violent, intoxicated, sad, etc...and this allows evil entities to take you to the extreme of emotions, and sometimes makes you go after others, if you don't spiritually ask God to open your eyes to things within you emotionally, or from intoxicates that allow your mind to be influenced or taken over. These are seen, unseen and done daily in our lives. Ask God to help you resist and refrain from them (evil spirits).

What Happen To Traditional Marriage?

CHAPTER 42

In the early 1900s, marriage was considered a blessing from God. Two people coming together in the name of God with real plans to be together forever. Now it seems people marry for reasons other than God and both coming together honestly and for the same reasons. After a while, it seems people were marrying for the wrong reasons and they start to become enemies to each other after a period of time. Some short and some after a long period of time.

Now with jobs, with different people, with different feelings about life, and about being with someone forever, changes people perspective on even wanting to get married, or remaining married. Its hard to vent to a person, and seek advise from people who despises marriage in the first place, or they use their way of life to give advise on yours. A dog can't give a cat advice on how to cat, and a unmarried person can't give advice to a married person, and still be able to make it make sense. Now you got internet, social media, with people telling other people about ways to react to a failing marriage, by people who've never been married at all. People today have things breaking them away from the real meaning of marriage, and why we should get married in this world is turning away from marriage and changing it into a future Satan wants it, and that's make people separate, and man and women feeling like they don't need each other and multiple things to discourage people from marriage and being fruitful and multiply, like God commanded.

Things like single independence, transgendering, and homosexuality, all prevent man and women from

TUG OF WAR

bonding as one and multiplying. People with failing relationships basing their opinions on their misfortunes, and slowly encourage future generations to avoid marriage all together, and people already married run discontinue it, making people not want marriage at all.

The Family Structure Destroyed

CHAPTER 43

Under God, everybody knows that family is very important in the eyes of God. To have a man and a women become complete as one, when they come together, and then develop righteous fruit(children), out of their completeness and develop a whole family tree of good fruit. It seems like the more high-tech technology became, the more separate the family structure become. T.V. propaganda started encouraging things such as rebellious children going against the natural order of the family structure (tradition). Giving children another ideology to utilize, meaning, Satan showed us as a child watching T.V., another choice to consider, by showing other children who are reading a script written by a hidden hand (Satanic guidance), who's showing kids how to decide matters that a child shouldn't even have an opinion on as a child. This started a revolution of teen rebelliousness, which encouraged teens to turn on their parents if they chose to. Then came the computers, laptops, and phones, that took this agenda to a whole new level. Once technology (Satan's creation) entered everybody's homes or handed it instantly began to separate the family members who seemed to want to be alone, on their journey through the portal they've entered thru technology, as being under a form of hypnosis. People will scatter to their own little corner in the house somewhere and drop their head down and enter this technological portal, no longer even seeing eye to eye, because even as a child, their journeying off seeking their own likes and dislikes, shaping themselves to be whatever catches the eyes of the beholder. Sadly, before you know it, your child has become something, or into something you'd never believe and we slowly but solely separated ourselves from family! Without even knowing it, or intentionally doing it, therefore destroying our very own family structure, all due to technology, (A Satanic tool created to destroy the family structure).

Satan's Promise

CHAPTER 44

One thing I would like people understand is that God in Heaven is real! We are all his creation, and Satan is an open enemy to God, and his creation (Adams seed), as we upgrade through life, we are shown that with Satan is an open enemy to The Most High and us. That his promise to destroy God's creation and the earth is not only in existence, but has been going on since the beginning of human kind, and is still happening today.

The Most High said to be fruitful and multiply, and to take care of, and preserve the earth, cause the earth will provide us with everything we need to live. With that being said, if God told us to do these things, then what would an enemy of God do. The answer would be to eliminate that which God said to do. From the beginning, Satan has been persuading people to sacrifice children, abortion, homosexuality, and transgender, etc... All in the cause to prevent God's children from multiplying. and now where coming into a time of artificial intelligence, to where people won't even be people anymore.

DNA splicing with animals, and other things, slowly erasing human DNA and Satan also has his aim at destroying the earth. Cutting down all the trees and forest to build highways, buildings, factories and in the process killing off the insects, and animals. Chemicals in the air to destroy the ozone layer. Chemicals buried in the ground, tainting the land's growth. Weapons of mass destruction, causing radiation, that poisons the earth and its inhabitants. Wars all over the world poisoning and killing constantly. Countries watching countries starve to death no water to drink. Now ask yourself, is Satan keeping his promise to come after humanity, and the earth. Just check ancient history up until now, cause the answer has always been there, and the Holy Scriptures. (watch the cartoon "The Lorax").

War

CHAPTER 45

I named this chapter "War"; to let people know what state of mind the world is in. You'd have to ask yourself why would a world that claims people come in peace, as well as the religions they participate in, show the total opposite of what they proclaim. If we know that God ordered us to be peaceful, and love one another, and want for your brother, what you'd want for yourself. Then that means someone is orchestrating the world to do the opposite (Satan). The same people who will lock their own citizens up for killing, and gangbanging, will send innocent troops, trained to kill sent over to a country to kill innocent women and children, without caring of any value of life. Have you ever wondered who's even given these people the knowledge to create such destruction on innocent people (Satan whispers the way to these people). Only people with spiritual evil would commit such acts for self-gain and say their doing it for the freedom of the United States and at the same time messing over their own citizens, who never wanted to go to war in the first place. Only Satan would have people all over the world using their intellect to create weaponry to eliminate life, either by chemicals in food fluoride in water, nuke bombs, etc..., and when it seems like times should be getting better, a hidden hand is aimed at making us destroy each other (Satan), the evil one is given control of the earth for a period of time, and he's using that time to whisper destruction to us. Satan is raging war on God's creation, (Adams seed's) humankind. In this way we will know it's a never-ending war on us but committed by us.

Divide & Conquer

CHAPTER 46

One of Satan's many tools is to divide and conquer. In doing so, you divide them, take out one and then take out the other. This tool is very easy to use cause its a strategy that ignites, and blows up on its own, Satan just instigate its beginning. All thru history, the same strategy has been used to get man to self-destruct since the beginning. Starting in the Garden of Eden, Satan divided Adam and Eve from God's instructions, and then Adam and Eve from each other. Every since then it's been many different ways we've been divided as a people on earth (God's Creations). Things like ethnicity religion, rich against poor, gangs, country against country, state against state, tribe against tribe, children against adults, and Gods creation against Satan's inventions (mixing DNA, cloning to put demons in flesh and technology). Ask yourself how can a world upgrade spiritually, if so many things are dividing mankind. No matter how anyone looks at it, Satan has influence on everything that makes someone hate, for the simple things people hate for nowadays, just cause of the color of their skin, or cause they think their religion is better. Killing over colors, neighborhoods, or causing the armed forces of our countries, and breeding these behaviors into our children, making them change the natural unprejudiced love they're born with their born with, being taught what and how to hate. Regardless of these things. Know this, Satan is aiming at all of us and don't care about none of the nonsense were dividing ourselves over, cause he aims to destroy all humankind as a whole, (wake up), and realize were all creations of The Most High. Togetherness and love is the only key.

Sometimes Satan Uses Family & Friends to Break Your Faith

A person starts walking on a spiritual road, Satan tries his best to challenge your faith, but when that doesn't work, it seems like he uses family and friends, that means that they might not even know their doing it intentionally, but through the whispers and actions of Satan. Family and friends are the perfect weapons to use cause they know just about everything about you, as far as the good and bad habits. They can get right next to you constantly. For instance, have you ever woken up and saying that you're gonna give up certain bad behaviors, that are pulling you down and then before you know it. A family member or friend appears to tempt you immediately. You stop drinking, and someone pops up with a bottle offering you some. Same thing with drugs, cigarettes, and when I stop eating pork, (which God ordains us not to eat) people still tried to entice me with eating some.

The same things can be said about violence, lust, and anything else that will lure you off your spiritual road to God. Many times, has it been said that when Satan can't get you directly, he will use other instruments to weaken you, being God's creation, we have to ask The Heavenly Creator to give us the strength to not only see these things as they come, but also the strength to overcome them.

When Religion Fails (You & God One On One)

CHAPTER 48

Many people go through a lot of ups and downs with their religions. A lot of times, they come back and forth to them or sometimes they change and enter another religion altogether. Know this, even without having a religion, people should know that God also said that he has a connection to each and every one of us (people are God's temple), our real relationship with God has always been a spiritual one on one with The Most High. Many times, we do it off instinct, like when you're in danger, you call for God's protection, or when you're locked up, you ask God to help prevent you from breaking down and going crazy. Know that by doing good, and treating others as you would want to be treated, or admitting the oneness of God in your one-on-one, is a personal religion with God, and the meeting is within the real temple (your mind), and that was the first religion in the beginning, Adam and Eve believed in one creator, Abraham believed in one creator, the Israelites and Islam (The Ismaelites), which come through Abraham sons, and the belief in one creator and nobody else.

Satan Started Attacking What Got Me Closer To God

We moved on the westside of Flint, and I got out of jail with an upgrade on spirituality, everything seemed to feel and be alright. We were in a new place people and police didn't know us, and I could feel that things could get better. I had my family and a safe place for my kids to come be with me on the regular. I would show them the things on the internet, T.V., and cartoons, that were occultist, and inspired by Satan, and his followers. No matter where you go and what you do, Satan will come for you in any way he can get in and divide what makes you strong in your faith. Nicole had got a job at the corner store in the neighborhood we'd moved in, the problem with this is whenever we'd have problems, she'd go to her new friends she met, that wasn't out for her best interest. The advice (Satan's whispers), these chicks were given her, had also given Satan a chance to intervene and cause chaos. In between her alcoholic problems, and new friends given her advice creating chaos over and over, to the point when she drink, you could see the evil in her. It got to the point where it was hard to be around her when she drank. We began to argue and fight a lot. Although I know you shouldn't put your hands on women, it was hard dealing with an alcoholic. It got to the point where we ended up splitting up cause I knew I would end up hurting her if it continued any further.

She moved in with a chick she met on the West, and during this divide and conquer situation, Satan made sure our family wouldn't get back together again. Satan through her friend Janie had her turning on family and friends. She began entrusting everything into her new crowd of people she assumed had her back and she turned on everyone who really did. While the drinking got worse, so did the relationship we had, had came to an end also, to the point she couldn't be trusted, cause she was so influenced by alcohol and fake friend Janie, who made it her business to destroy everything Nicole had going for her, just so she would have to depend on Janie only, and Satan came in full charge.

After moving in with Janie, my kids told me they didn't like living there and they didn't like Janie either. Nicole's decision making took her not only down, but backwards. Nicole began to blame me for the split up cause I was constantly cheating on her, had a baby on her, ever spent time, or did things with her. Along with the fights, these things we'd already had gotten over, and the more she'd talk about these things, the more you could tell it was all coming from her friend Janie, who'd already lost her older son to her baby daddy and couldn't really maintain her household with her young son. She desperately needed Nicole to even keep her head above water. Nicole fell for this scheme, and it destroyed our family instantly, and the alcohol (Satan), made sure it stayed this way.

A Thin Line Between Family & Sin

CHAPTER 50

When you're with someone for about twelve years, and have children together, it tears your soul apart when it is separated from you, cause what balances you out in God, is a strong balance that guides you naturally from God himself. It has meaning to your soul and guides your right and wrong nature. However, I felt she was wrong by allowing herself to be influenced by her new crowd and her alcohol problem. I had also blamed myself for the other half of this and when this all happened. It hit me hard because you want to help, but alcoholism is a deadly disease that will poison all who are forced to witness it.

Alcoholism tore my heart apart to have to watch her deteriorate right before my eyes, especially after witnessing her mother die from alcohol, and she inherited this curse, but I could not let my two youngest daughters be victimized by her choices to get help with the drinking, and them being over there with Janie, who they didn't like, or liked being there. Bottom line, I always loved her but these things through my balance off and Satan made sure it didn't come together again. Though we were still spending a lot of time together, with plans of trying to get back together. It just seemed like it was becoming harder and harder, to the point of seeming impossible. Satan through the whispers of her new friends destroyed this peace of mind. It also destroyed our children's connection to her, cause they didn't like Janie, or being there.

The more time apart, made us both go backwards. With no kids being home, my day consisted of selling dope, and back hanging out, getting away from a neighborhood I wasn't from, and didn't trust the people there, especially since me and her fell out, and her friend Janie was trying to get these dudes to get at me. Her drinking got worse and the children's relationship with her got worse also, they felt she was allowing her roommate Janie to mess over them and wouldn't stand up for them just to keep a roof over her head.

The more this elevated, the family structure slowly came crashing down and the worst things that came from seeing my children go through this, made me aim at taking the kids from her. She didn't work, couldn't take care of the kids, stayed drunk all the time, hanging out with Janie, leaving the kids to watch themselves. She was failing as a mother and refused to change and wouldn't give the girls to me just to spite me. The environment they were in made me feel she was giving up on our children and I refused to watch

my daughters be around an environment she had
them in.

My Feelings of Giving Up

Satan found what tools he could use to destroy my family, he continued to use these tools to create chaos. Her friend Janie not only was influencing her, but also started stirring up problems between me and dudes from the westside, who didn't like me cause I was from Beecher, which is affiliated with the Vice Lords and Bloods, and from Janie and Nicole constantly telling our business to these other friends of her and Janie, that they would make comments that could only had come from them. Nicole being the drunk she was, would never take responsibility for the chaos her and Janie started, or even telling Janie to mind her own business. I started making sure I kept a heater on me. The tension in the air was thick.

Satan had created a chaotic situation back in my life, that had me back on tip, something I hadn't had to do in years. My spirituality had fell back down. I didn't trust nobody around the area, Nicole and even Nicole's two sons, who seem to be reporting to Nicole and Janie, as to when I was home ,or not, and if it wasn't for my daughters telling me about all these things, I would have been in the dark to what was coming my way, and Nicole knew these dudes were going to try to get me if they could.

Unfortunately, it got me to the point of breaking down, cause I couldn't believe she let all this get orchestrated, from some people she barely knew. Me being how I am got ready for war before they could get me. Satan had gotten the chance to turn my life back into a warzone, with no family, no peace of mind and this had taken me far from God and back into Satan's hand and this situation became me mentally, and then physically. I was back to my lower self again fully.

Visions of Future Destruction

───────── ✦ ─────────

CHAPTER 52

Being back at a savage, low state of mind, you would
think that would have been gave up on me as being a
lost cause, but instead, The Most High showed
me a vision of a future event that I didn't understand. I
had the chance to go to Texas, to spend Thanksgiving
my mother and get away from the madness, but for
some reason, I decided to stay. During the vision, I
had a dream of me, my stepson day-day looking at
what appeared to be four funeral hearses, and one
trailing the others. I saw three different showings of
the end of 2018. Me and Nicole was talking, and I told
her about the dream, she told me it was a vision of

her death, but I told her I felt it was about me, cause all the drama that was on the floor with me and these others dudes. I felt something might pop off before the end of this year. Nicole had invited to their Thanksgiving meal, cause her and the kids wanted me to come, seeming like things might smooth over and get better as far as the beefing, but not knowing it would be our last meal between all of us.

Destruction Came

CHAPTER 53

On Thanksgiving, and the weekend after, it seemed like our family healing was not far away. Like the old saying goes, once it's written in Gods books, it's signed, sealed, and delivered. December 3, 2018, I got a call from the school, who said they needed to talk to Nicole about the kids' dress code being violated and the amount of absences they had. We'd just texting each other recently, but Nicole didn't pick up, so I went over there during arriving, and chaos erupted! Somebody end up getting shot,/the vision became real, God had revealed it to me months before it happened. I had felt it within and it was bothering, and it was bothering me for months, and when I had the vision. God was revealing a horrific event that was to come, and change my life forever, in a form of shock, I took off, and left the scene like everyone else.

TUG OF WAR

Satan Won't Stop

After getting everything illegal out of the house and hiding it in an abandoned house. I felt the world as I knew it was over. All the things I worked for, the large family I asked God to bless me with. Now I was alone in an abandoned house left miserably to myself, knowing when they get me, I might be blamed for this. My phone was turned off so no one could trace it, no one to call, no one there to talk to. Man, every police in Flint looking for me. Satan had tried and tried to get me away from God, so he could take me down, and I felt like he finally did. I was alone freezing in this abandoned house, with nowhere to go, and no one who could change the situation. I let down God, I didn't even have the guts to ask him for help.

I had finally let Satan pull me all the way down. I was actually feeling like I was in hell on earth, mentally and physically. Thoughts of suicide hit my mind, cause at the age I was at I felt like I couldn't take anymore and when you feel like that, only two things hit your mind, suicide, which I don't ever feel I could strengthen myself for this type of sin, or shoot it out. This showed me that there's no limit to what Satan will try to get you to do. Which pulls you all the way down, and when you get there, he'll even try to convince you to go and take yourself out. Suicide is a major sin!

God Never Left Me

Just as I had thoughts of giving up, I heard whispers in my mind saying don't give up, even though I had already done it, because everyone was scared to let me

hide at their place cause every police in Flint was looking for me. I couldn't fault them at all, but something told me to cut on my phone, and as soon as I did, I seen my mother had texted me saying "Call ASAP!" I did. As soon as she answered, she asked me was I alright and what happened? I told her that while going over there to talk to Nicole about the school calling, her roommate's boyfriend was there, and we got into it, and he ended up getting shot twice, and he jumped through a window in the house to escape, while everyone ran from the scene. My mother hurt because she felt Nicole was the person responsible for all this drama and eventually my downfall. She felt that it would be better for me to fight my case and live than run and end up getting killed by police. The same thoughts going on in my mind, to not run. I couldn't see turning myself into police, but I came out of the abandoned house and caught the bus to my own hood (Beecher). I didn't find anybody to hook up with, so I called my second oldest daughter Takoya and she told me she and my stepson Tyquan were on their way to get me.

The Last Meal With Loves Ones

Never in a million years would I'd thought under circumstances like this, that the ones to come to the rescue to assist me would be the kids (Takoya and Tyquan, and they friend Nicole), who'd been looking for me for two days, but I had my phone off. They said they figured I was hiding somewhere, which I was hiding in abandoned house. They came to pick me up off a street I told them I was on in Beecher, and we went back to my daughter's apartment, finally being able to get a little peace in days, I passed out due to exhaustion of hiding and freezing in the abandoned house.

Most people wanted by police everywhere always wish they had a chance to talk with ones, eat a last meal, or just say your last peace before going away for what might be the rest of your life. Somehow, someway (God) gave me a chance to do it, and everyone wandered how I evaded being caught, seconds after the shooting.

I ran home got all the stuff out and as soon as I jumped the fence and made it to the abandoned house, the SWAT team state police, Flint police, and the sheriff's department ran up in the house, and after exiting the house, they surrounded the westside, with police cause they knew I was still in the area. I turned my phone off, and eventually made it off the westside, to Beecher, then to my daughters, and with the guidance of God. I got to spend the new year of 2019 with my children, with the help of my baby mother Shenina and my older children, I was able to talk or see my younger children, some on cell phone face chat, that even know I was there, cause I couldn't let them see me cause they momma (Nicole). Might have been around I had meetings with my homeboy Triggaman, to put him up on what had happened, and my boy D Stan, who like Trigg was putting stuff together for me, and preparing me for whatever, cause I was put on Crime Stoppers, and all the news.

My brother Howard also snuck out to see me. All the people to talk to under situations like this was my mother, cause it never fails to hear God's voice through the voice of your mother, who'd not only supplied me with money to survive for the moment, but also to put my total trust in God, to get me through this, by fighting the situation in court and not on the streets, or allowing police to try to kill me. I got the chance to tell my older children that no matter what happens to me, to keep faith in God and the blessings of togetherness with their brother and sisters. For them to be ready to get their younger sisters if the time came. God gave me time to spend with my loved ones and study my case. On January 23, 2019, the task force started going house to house of who was close to me. When they got to my baby mother Shenina, he called our daughter, and said we might be next. Gods warning to man up, or create more chaos, by waiting to see if they were gone run up in my daughter's spot, with my grandson Messiah being there also.

My daughter to get evicted due to harboring a fugitive, so by having a head start. I decided to come out in the open and I kissed my daughter and my grandson and told her everything was gone be alright. After walking towards the gas station to get some squares, I could see trucks posted up on each block I walked past. The Marshall's posted up all around. I went into the gas station so they would have to arrest me in public, to prevent being shot and they came in, called me by name and arrested me, and took me to Flint County Jail, where I would begin the biggest fight of my life.

My Last Road

CHAPTER 57

After getting to the county jail, the only thing I could think about was my case, and never being able to see my kids again. Just when you start to feel like Satan has won, and your life has just gone to hell, God started strengthening me with my own thoughts, and other people telling me to put my faith in God, and not up. I started reading the Bible and Quran and talking to people about spirituality. It's as if God wanted me to know that whatever circumstances I'm under, to not let it interfere with me reaching to God and asking him for help. I always knew how to direct people to God, but with the ups and downs of my own life, needed help myself through God, to uplift myself, along with these other brothers looking for the same healing. They say God makes things happen for a reason, and I was beginning to awaken to what he's always tried to get me to focus on, and take me away from what had me at a standstill of reaching him. I stop letting this situation move me away from God and made myself move closer to him.

I started talking more about God, and ways for me and the brothers in here to stay in God's grace, no matter what the outcome of our situations. Before I knew it, certain things started turning for the better in my case. Just like always, Satan will try to the best of his abilities to stop you on your Godly road, a deputy for no reason, tried to put me in a cell with a brother known to be jumping on people's cases. I refused and got put in the hole for 15 days, which end up given me the alone time with myself and God that I needed anyway. Breaking down one night thinking to myself of never being able to be with family again, I asked God to strengthen me through this, because it was beginning to be too much for me to bear mentally. After doing my 15 days in the hole, I was put on the floor with a lot of younger people. When I thought it was a bad situation to be put on a floor full of younger people anyway. God showed me how he is the best of planners, in any situation. What I thought was bad by being put on this floor, ended up being a floor full of young wild men, who very much wanted and needed spiritual help. Me and a brother name Rico started hack group meetings at a table, that started bringing lots of other brothers to walking that spiritual road. The moral of this story ain't about whether I beat this case, or go to prison, but knowing that God is real.

Whenever Satan tempts you to do wrong, seek refuge in The Most High, live your life striving to do right during your good times and your bad times. Everybody in life has a story of ups and downs, while searching for God. He's always been their waiting for us all. From Adam and Eve to you and I. All praise is due to The Most High, who had to take me away from things pulling me down, even a situation like this has a reason to bring a person back to God, where we belong.

Share Your Road To GOD With Another

---◦×◦---

I wrote this chapter so everyone who reads this knows to share any and all knowledge about God. And to start making a close relationship with him, when in trouble, in hard times and even when you're not. Religion shows you roads to The Most High. There's only one creator, and people in the Bible and Quran are people like us, they didn't use a name when it came to what people consider to be religion, they called it the way of life (the Deen), as it is still today called in (Islam), and you learn how to make it your way of life, and not just saying I got a religion. People back then had the same ups and downs, spiritually, and somehow found their way to The Most High, who seems to be already waiting. Commandments are demands from God that normally we should be already doing. If a person is hungry, feed them. If their thirsty, give them something to drink. Teach someone who has no knowledge of God, teach them about God.

Treat people with kindness, it doesn't matter what color or creed. Give the same love and respect that you would want. There's no such thing as a reason for war, so avoid it if possible. Stop the things that take you out of Godliness and avoid things you should know are satanically motivated.

We are in a period of time where Satan is turning everything ungodly, and making it look normal, generation by generation, and it only gets worse. By no means am I judging anyone especially from the things I've done in my lifetime. But to fully understand what God is to show us, we must also open our eyes and mind to what Satan is trying to do to us, and the world. Love and togetherness are a couple of the tools we need being God's creation. In order to fight Satan, along with the shield of God. As long as things can separate us, Satan is winning. The world is becoming hellish and Satanic and were letting it happen. We're being put to sleep by Satan.

I've finally reached a point in my life spiritually to understand what God wanted for me this whole time, and as I ran from him (God), so many times before, and been forced to crawl back to him humbling myself. God knows what the future has in store for us. Things happen for a reason, you must meet people certain people for a reason and sometimes we have to go through certain things for a reason. So, in that, we read examples and also become examples for those having a hard time finding their road to The Most High. Yeshua (so-called Jesus), came to remind first, the lost tribe of

Isreal, Ismaelites both seeds of Abraham, then all, how to love one another, cause hate will make your mind and body become such.

Angels and Demons are constantly around, and we have the will to allow possession of both in us. We have to control what we do, what we react to, and avoid what opens are vessels, inviting bad entities in, who are awaiting such invitations. We have to show children that God really exists and help children without parents, or lack of one know that someone does care, and to not give up on their belief in God, and life itself.

Even if someone is homeless and without money, engage in conversation with them and offer them food, as you might be interacting with one of God's angels. All these things are subjects of either things we've went through, or asked God to help, or forgive us for. So, praise God, and love one another, and like the famous words in the movie "The Wizard of Oz",

TUG OF WAR

stay on the yellow brick road (God's road), and may God continue to have mercy on us all.

Peace, blessings & love!

Conclusion

As I overlook my life and all my ups and downs. I've come to realize that God has directed my life the whole time, and it was meant for me to go through the trials, and tribulations I went through. The people chosen by God to show me the road to him. Some people judge others due to a person jumping off this road many times, but a true God inspired person knows that is a never-ending battle, which Satan will come for you, all your life, no matter what.

Experience shows a person this, especially people who've had ups and downs with this most of their lives and found out God was still there waiting to help. I've seen angels, and demons, fiery chariots (UFO), had visions, premonitions of death, births, and chaotic events. Yet, I still managed to jump off the road to The Most High, over and over again. It never stopped The Most High from revealing things to me. People will be tested by Satan and the many things that can lure you off your road. Things like drugs, drinking, lust, violence, anger, jealousy, and many more. I've struggled all my life with the goods and bass of this wicked world. This road of mine has shown me how to defeat Satan, through God's power and grace. I understand now that it was decisions I've made, people I shouldn't have been around. Chasing riches the wrong way. Being with women for the wrong reasons, and not real love, messed over the ones who deserved real love. I know now that this last relationship would've been the death of me. God took me away from the person who had me going backwards, and the evil that surrounded her. In that way, I could work on my own short comings, in my life. I look back on Satan, and my old life and prepare to run to my new life with God.

- Acknowledgments -

I would first like to thank first and foremost God Almighty the Creator of All, who created and formed me in the womb. Who knew from the beginning this would be.

To my mother, Beatrice Johnson, who has always been my source of strength, my teacher, and guiding light throughout my life. You never doubted my good abilities, even when I didn't believe I had any. Words could never describe my love for you, and the importance of you being in my life. Being a single mother, you still stood strong for us and always told us to keep God in our lives, no matter what. Through my good and bad, I've always prayed for God to put me in a position to be the man you had faith in, me becoming.

- Dedication -

I Dedicate This Book to With Unconditional Love.

To my brothers, Paul, Leon, Courntney, Howard (Rest peacefully big bro), and Deshawn. MY LOVE IS NEVER ENDING!

To the mothers of my beautiful children, Shermaine Carroll, Shenina Peoples, Kristen Dunnings, Nicole Watson (may God bless you, rest good baby girl), and Deanna Ghinelli. Through the ups and downs and pain I've caused, or we caused each other. I never meant to hurt you all and hope y'all will forever forgive me. Lord knows it's been a long hard bumpy road dealing with me and you all will forever be a piece of my life, no matter what. I will forever cherish the good times and hope y'all forgive me for the bad. Y'ALL WILL ALWAYS BE APART OF MY LIFE.

To my children, Andreada, Takoya, Geneva, Teron Jr., Treyshawn, Nikiyah, Dominic, and Sakara.
Please Learn From Me & Be Better Than!

To the children I raised as my own, Deonta, Tyquan, Ashawta, Tavis, Dayshawn, & Daviyonna.
Y'ALL WILL ALWAYS BE CHILDREN OF MINE!

To my grand babies, the next generation, I love y'all so deeply.

To my family, Ann and James Walker (grandparents), My Aunts: Betty, Pearl, Jamese (R.I.P. beautiful), My cousins: Tria, Wiesel, Moses, Zariah, Michael, and all of their children. I Have Unconditional Love For You All.

The Johnson family, Uncle Haywood (R.I.P.), Aunt Darlene (R.I.P.) My cousins: Tia, Dolly (R.I.P), Fuzzy, Viva, Venus, Vance (R.I.P.), Shawn, Latrese and their children. I LOVE YOU!

To the peoples of Richard family, y'all are forever engraved in my heart.

To the entire Beecher community! BUC-LUV

To everyone whose made a positive impact on my life, on the streets, in prison, or just wishful thinking. Love is love under God!

Last, but not least to the entire city of Flint. May God protect us from water contamination that's ever so present still to this day. Still, we rise stronger than ever!

TUG OF WAR

TUG OF WAR

COMING SOON

"Buried Alive: It's My Story, Let Me Tell It"
The Sequal

7

Made in the USA
Columbia, SC
08 August 2024